for Emma and Gaspar

"The understanding of cities is related to the transcription of their images, proffered as in a dream." Siegfried Kracauer

Mapping HONG KONG

Laurent GUTIERREZ and Valérie PORTEFAIX

edited by ANNA KOOR   foreword by ACKBAR ABBAS

Designed by MAP OFFICE

The project "mapping HK" was presented at the 7th Venice Architecture Biennale,
on the theme, "The City: Less Aesthetic, more Ethic" - June 2000/October 2000.

For details about MAP OFFICE visit: http://www.map-office.com

FIRST EDITION
ISBN 962-86040-1-5

Published in HK by   **map book**

Color Separation Film by   **Leung Yau Graphic Arts Agency**

Printed in HK by   **Gear Printing Limited**

Ackbar Abbas

Re-cognising the city

On arrival at a new destination, tourists are typically given a map to help them find their way around the city.

Not being able to find one's way, the non-tourist Walter Benjamin writes, is uninteresting and banal. But then, he goes on to say, the art of losing one's way in the city is an altogether different matter, and requires a different kind of map. This is the sort of map that Gutierrez and Portefaix attempt to provide in their book *mapping HK*. It is a map more for residents than for tourists; a paradoxical map that "makes strange" a city that has grown too familiar, to reveal a city we only half know; an intricately drawn map that enables us – to stray. And it is Hong Kong (as it was Paris for the German writer Benjamin) that has taught these two French architects/authors the art of straying.

For their task, Gutierrez and Portefaix have devised an innovative method based on both rationality and chance.

They have invented a text that proceeds, at the level of content, by way of images, captions, quotations and discursive argument. This part of the method is akin to collage, where the disparate elements sometimes reinforce, sometimes subvert, one another. We are given the impression of an unpredictable field, with "lines of flight" taking off in different directions. However, if this sounds chaotic, we have only to turn to the second level, the level of structure, to see how rigorously the whole is organised. The unpredictable field is crossed (and cross-referenced) by six grids, themselves fluid and flexible, with two-word titles like "fluid machine" or "soft disappearance". These grids (which are also chapter headings) have, it should be noted, the status not of fixed theses but of working hypotheses. They are like so many probes into the unknown, devices by means of which the spatial unconscious of the city could be glimpsed in its details. Each grid is like a dice-throw; and as the French poet Mallarmé has reminded us, a throw of the dice never did abolish chance.

Each chapter of the book approaches the city at an angle, often an unexpected one, as if to catch it unawares, to map it napping. This play of prospectives, this cat-and-mouse game, is exhilarating enough in itself, but it also implies something else: a sense that Hong Kong's spatial complexity cannot be directly reproduced, only seduced, through patience, guile and intuitive understanding. Accordingly, the authors have created a seductive visual and verbal text which, like the city itself, could be entered into at any point. The organisation of the text is paratactic rather than syntactic. The authors do not place themselves in the position of the omniscient narrator with a panoptic view of the action, but present themselves as participant observers engaging in a multi-voiced dialogue with the city.

In spite of the multiple perspectives, each chapter does have a focus and so does the book as a whole; and it falls on the new social spaces produced by the rapid pace of economic and technological changes. As yet, our sense of these spaces is sufficiently bedazzled for us to experience them still with a mixture of fascination and unease. A case in point is the Mid-levels escalator, the world's longest, a kind of electric ladder that connects the Mid-levels to Central. In the chapter "Dynamic Labyrinth", the escalator is described almost as a kind of metallic snake that moves people along as if by peristalsis. The city as machine takes on a horrifying organic quality, like the prophetic images that we find in horror movies such as *Alien*. Unlike in Alien though, there is only a hint of horror here, but it is enough to suggest that in our experience of Hong Kong as city – increasingly described since 1997 as a "global city" – the sense of greater interconnectedness brought about by technology goes together with a sense of disorientation. And this perhaps is one of the ways in which "globalism" is experienced at a local level. In this regard, we can cite another movie, less melodramatic and closer to home, namely, Wong Kar-wai's urban romantic comedy *Chungking Express*, where the mid-level escalator plays a crucial role in dramatising Hong Kong as a social space where interconnectedness produces proximity without intimacy. In all this, what we are given to see is a process in which the organic itself gives way to "the sex appeal of the inorganic".

Ultimately then, the city poses a problem in epistemology more than anything else: it challenges our pretensions to know it. Throughout the book, the authors present us with a series of fugitive and diverse cityscapes, but these are cityscapes that threaten to escape our visual and conceptual grasp. For example, in "Running Scape", they show how new buildings materialise on old sites. Their impact on us as urban spectacles sometimes makes us forget that they are also the instruments of speculative investment. The spectacle masks the speculation, as the visible city co-exists uneasily with the invisible city. Or in "Chip Planning", they invoke the image of the *Plug-in City*, where buildings are like fungible electronic chips in a computer board whose language is not more intelligible than hieroglyphics even for those who use it. And in "Appropriated Space", they show how changes in city space break down our understanding of public and private, as private capital appropriates more of public space for its own ends – for "publicity", for example. However the book is not just saying that the city is incomprehensible. It is saying rather that to understand the city today, we will need to change our images of it.

Nowhere is this more clearly implied than in the final chapter entitled "Soft Disappearance". A dominant image of Hong Kong is that it is constantly remaking itself, ruthlessly cancelling out the past and moving on, creating a *tabula rasa* on which to build anew. What the authors point out however is that the *tabula rasa* is always incomplete, there inevitably exists the remains of the day. They direct our attention to the moment between erasure and rebuilding when urban fragments are still visible – if only as ruins. Some of their examples are the Mai Po Marshes, the isolated walled villages, the small shops in the midst of high capital enterprises and so on. In their text, these urban leftovers serve something other than nostalgia. They are the fragments of history and memory that could form the basis of a hermeneutics of the city's future; a hermeneutics that is neither celebratory nor apocalyptic; a spatial hermeneutics that might allow us to re-cognise the city.

Gutierrez + Portefaix

Mapping Hong Kong

"The image of external things possesses for us the ambiguous dimension that in external natural, everything can be considered to be connected, but also as separated. The uninterrupted transformations of materials as well as energies bring everything into relationship with everything else and make one cosmos out of all the individual elements." Georg Simmel, *Bridge and Door*

This book begins with a primary impression: Hong Kong, a hyper-dense skyscraper forest located at the bottom of a mountainous jungle. A territory of 1,000 square kilometres, Hong Kong's evolution is barely fifty years "deep" apart from its small downtown with a hundred years or so of history and a few pockets of ancestry. Hong Kong is an instant urbanscape with instant architecture. Most of its buildings are less than ten years old and those are mostly of uniform type and cover the most recent strips of reclaimed land. Yet, this port city has a remarkable, even fascinating character to its urban form, which raises enough questions to challenge its *mapping*.

Tourists and foreigners share an ability to be constantly confused by the novelty. In that sense and contrary to the locals, they are only capable of grasping the surface of things, ie. an abstract image of reality. The contrast between the dense high-rise city and the natural island/mountain setting is so violent that an immediate understanding is apparent from this conflicting and evident juxtaposition.

Beyond the visible, there is the expression of a concentrated community defined by cultural, historical, geographical and sociological references. Even after recognising the social complexity, there is the problem of synthesising the mass without ignoring the particular. By omitting precise chronology and statistical data, a further reading of the city conveys an intense and complicated network of personal intentions, historical memory and oblivion, conscious and unconscious factors at collective and individual levels.

A sensation of vertigo finally fixes the image of a difficult and ever changing territory. Acceleration and the absence of transition produce an ephemeral spark of moments (not necessarily events) that emphasise the conceptual tension of everyday life. These experiences are translated into a choreography of movement, that recaptures the rhythm of Hong Kong life - the overwhelming traffic, crowds, and the unexpected occurrence.

The object of this book is to unfold this apparent complexity and represent it from new perspectives. Hong Kong can only be comprehended in a collage of different perceptions, such as the search for synthesised relations, the nature of continuity and rupture, and the recuperation of the individual within the social group. A new classification develops in the form of a non-exhaustive inventory – a collection of human activities in relation to the technological revolution, economic globalisation, and cultural change.

At this point, a parenthesis can introduce a brief comparison between Paris and London at the turn of the 20th century, and Hong Kong at the switch to the 21st. Both European cities became centres for exchange and markets for luxury goods at a moment when the dimensions of their territories and populations exploded. Their mutation was not marked by quantitative blasts but rather by the qualified organisation of multiple forces - a financial structure, a market and a political centre. Their essence was manifested as multi-articulated urban types, incorporating a system that would generate a comprehensive service network to support their growth. Following these outlined observations, Hong Kong's contemporary evolution appears to be relevant enough to draft the comprehension of a new emerging urbanity.

"A port city that used to be located at the intersections of different spaces, Hong Kong will increasingly be at the intersections of different times or speed." Ackbar Abbas, Hong Kong - *Culture and the Politics of Disappearance*

The question of space, place, and also the particular pressure of accelerated time, make Hong Kong a unique moving platform of exchange within both the Asian and world markets. During its early colonial period it was an emporium, then in the 1950's Hong Kong became a competitive factory, and now it has developed a new competitive force as a centre of a global information system. Since 1997, the territory has rapidly acquired a high potential for experimentation and the development of extreme conditions. This implies that Hong Kong's urban structure can still incorporate the latest economic changes and strategies.

Because of its particular history and geography, Hong Kong represents a unique synthesis of both global city and local territory. Globalisation contributes to the wide diffusion of economic activities while intensifying centralisation and the tendency towards centralised control. The rapid development of "exchangers" - centres as platforms for exchange - has led many observers to assert that the effectiveness of Hong Kong's urban phenomena lies in its economic multiplicity and intensity. For example, Hong Kong's Central Business District (CBD) constitutes only one centre among many others.

The new airport core programme, the container terminal, the current Cyberport development and the future Disneyland project are also specific competitive international centres which rely on the capacity for global production, communication and control. However from a local perspective, geography, history and culture continue to play an important role in giving shape and qualification to this new strategic network.

This disposition raises questions concerning economic and social evolution since most of Hong Kong's urban environment gives shape to these transformations. Limited territory has given planners an opportunity to avoid the conformities of centralised and linear growth, and encouraged a diversified and complicated territorial system. Instead of a homogeneous city, there are a multiplicity of archipelagos that are connected by an efficient network of communication and transport infrastructure. Together, these fragments form an original approach towards the "urban-territorial" scale, where the presence of mountains and the harbour is also implicated. The particular hybrid conditions of the territory can be seen in its physical reality as well as in its representation. On the one hand, its global condition provides some explanation of how the entire environment - urban or not – definitely responds to a critical number of dual conditions: simultaneity and speed, multiplicity and flexibility, uncertainty and the ephemeral. On the other hand, typical images of Hong Kong expose a series of discordant and contrasting forms, ranging from the chaotic and hybrid arrangements of streets, to the sharp line that cuts the urban fringe from its natural surroundings.

Local context and global conditions conjointly direct the multiple spaces through which urbanisation is constituted. In this context and at any level, Hong Kong's evolution appears as a perfect expression of continuous movement, a moving plate-form between local and global scenarios. In terms of planning strategies, these observations have direct consequences that can be interpreted through mapping.

Mapping

"Make a map, not a reproduction." Deleuze and Guattari, *Mille Plateaux*

Mapping aims to unravel the multi-dimensional tensions that spread across the surface of Hong Kong and attempts to code an all-embracing vision. A new critical instrument was developed to observe the current urban explosion, one that is capable of simultaneously exposing the abstract (global) and the particular (local). Today many proposals require architects and planners to jointly seek new instruments for approaching territorial

movements, and to represent and conceive new urban dimensions. Aerial photography and thematic cartography allow access to some viewpoints from which visible phenomena can be captured. As an autonomous
discipline, traditional cartography gained recognition for its practical uses in navigation, logistics and further
conquests. It is also a primary instrument for political, military and economic operations. Learning from ancient
maps tells us more about the perception of a territory than about its factual constitution. Using simplified
codes, they present a diagrammatic representation of its essence or a metaphoric reading of a place.

According to Gilles Deleuze and Felix Guattari, a map is not the reproduction of self enclosed unconsciousness, but
it does construct it. They explain that the principles of cartography contribute to the process of producing
rhizomorphic systems, and more precisely, to the transfer of information from one state to another over time.
Rather than linear growth, a rhizome possesses in its genetic structure the potential for self mutation.
Expressing a difference between cartography and tracing, they argue that a map discloses properties of open
structures. Based on these principles, a map is not a copy of reality but a proposal to re-invent it and to
project a given situation further. It can be seen as an extension of the system, ie. the further addition of
layers to represent an existing condition.

Using this definition, mapping is neither a fixed image of territory nor the stratification of visual contours, but the
projected image of its inherent mutation. This process does not result in an abstract project but the possible
development of the real. It is an open dynamic map capable of infiltrating reality and giving it new momen-
tum. Transportation and distribution, gravity and density, markets and economy are barometers that are simultaneously used for measuring amplitude, and for estimating the potential for subsequent planning. As a new
critical instrument for architects and planners, mapping is developed in order to interpret urban phenomena.
Hong Kong is used as a prototype to experiment with mapping.

Mapping Hong Kong

To participate in a new reading of Hong Kong, observers need to place a critical distance between their observation point and the global horizon. Avoiding the stereotypical opposition between local and global, they must accept the paradox and look at the two as one when observing urban phenomena through this new critical instrument. In this book, six interdependent vectors are identified. Together they produce an unfolding vision of future territorial strategies. Based on the analysis of economic, social and physical movements, these vectors first identify the nature (direction and orientation) of these movements accurately, then their intensity. The first vector directly refers to human, mechanical and information movements, and translates them into fluidity and acceleration.

The designation of "Fluid machine" suggests different layers of flows, supported by visible and invisible lines that are spread all over the territory. Particular attention is given to containers as vehicles for merchandise. The continuous movement of "boxes" between the harbour and road, produces an effervescent, unstable landscape.

"Running scape" is related to spatial mobility. The two-dimensional surface of the harbour, the floating pedestrian network, and the linear strips of new urban development, give Hong Kong a unique disposition from which to extend each of these potential planes. From that perspective, the future course of development seems to involve no obstacle or limits.

The third vector is "Chip planning". Interchange, flexibility and diversity give the architectural and urban project its specific form. Hong Kong remains a competitive centre since its territory can afford the continuous re-adaptation and replacement of buildings, blocks and major programmes. Like a computer, each component can be replaced with a more effective one, and the city is planned to achieve maximum performance.

A sensation of bewilderment, produced by the constant change of place and level, inspired "Dynamic labyrinth".

In Hong Kong, the pedestrian has to find a personal route through the density, cutting through atriums of buildings, using the elevated walkway network or the lift access to different levels of a building, and even the mountain's slopes. The multiplicity of options on offer is so large that everyone can experience the city in their own way.

"Appropriated place", the fifth vector, presents the blurring limits between what were formerly exclusively public or private spaces. Because it is neither public nor private, an appropriated place is occupied according to alternating circumstances. As opposite examples, a bank lobby can be made public under certain conditions, whereas a plaza may look public but does not allow anyone to freely use its space.

Lastly, "Soft disappearance" expresses the non-stop and violent decomposition of the territory, including the mountains, the harbour and an infinity of buildings. At different scales, both natural and human-made landscapes succumb to the constant pressure of accelerated time. However, it is rare to catch the moment of transition when these fragments are visible like traces or ruins, as a vacant plot is immediately reused, for example as a temporary parking lot, whilst anticipating its next mutation.

Illustrated by images, statements, captions and text, each vector reflects the energy that originates from its specific urban condition as a dialectical image of certain appearances and the projection of a forthcoming reality. In that sense, the vectors illustrate human activities, as well as their fantasies. For this purpose, the use of photography projects something in between hyper-reality and complete illusion, thus bearing its own aesthetic. This visual projection allows the multiplication of layers to embrace the maximum of information, including a further understanding of images, words, layers, paths, textures and all the substances that make Hong Kong.

FLUID-MACHINE EXPRESSES A DYNAMIC THAT IS SPECIFIC TO HONG KONG BECAUSE OF THE EXTREME LOCAL PHYSICAL CONDITIONS. TODAY THE CITY/TERRITORY IS AN AGGLOMERATION OF INTRICATELY INTERLOCKING SYSTEMS OF EXCHANGE WHICH HAVE EVOLVED VERY RAPIDLY. THE MOVEMENT OF PRODUCTS OR INFORMATION IS ORGANISED SEPARATELY FROM ALL HUMAN ACTIVITIES. WHETHER IT IS THE PHYSICAL SPACE OF THE CONTAINER OR THE DEMATERIALISED DOMAIN OF THE COMPUTER, ALL SERVE TO OPTIMISE THE COMPETITIVE SPEED OF THE MARKET. AS A RESULT MAN HAS LOST CONTROL, SUSPENDED IN A SYSTEM COMPLETELY DEPENDENT ON MACHINES.

Fluid machine

1

"I HAVE POINTED OUT ON PREVIOUS OCCASIONS THAT URBAN SPACE IS COMPOSED OF NOT ONLY IMMOVABLE OBJECTS SUCH AS BUILDINGS AND CIVIL ENGINEERING WORKS BUT VARIOUS THINGS IN FLOW SUCH AS WATER AND AIR, HUMAN BEINGS AND AUTO-MOBILES STIRRED BY DIVERSE ACTIVITIES, AND DIFFERENT KINDS OF ENERGY AND INFORMATION." Toyo Ito, "The City is a Garden of Microchips" (*JA Library*. n°2, summer 1993) Fluid machine refers to motion. In Hong Kong there is a continual fluctuation of people, goods, data and services as moving entities, together forming a society where the whole structure is in movement. This dynamic is supported by thousands of signs indicating both movement and intensity of urban flows. Each flow individually forms its own complex horizontal network, further linked vertically through different transportation systems. The transit of man and merchandise, the information infrastructure (system) for capital and technology, and virtual flows of information are the components of an invisible network emerging in specific places. Architecture of flow takes place at vertical junctions or points of turbulence. Like a traffic interchange, airport, train or subway station, port or ferry pier, each forms a specific network yet related to each other.

Fluid machine is perfectly adapted to Hong Kong's capitalist economy, which is part of the global market and its multiple decentralised circuits. For these reasons, Hong Kong is a major global centre where networks and flows are developed to the extreme. Both new infrastructures and the hyper-concentration of facilities create a strategic terrain for a network of international corporate cultures (international finance, telecommunications, information technology). These networks are open systems capable of absorbing new centres without causing instability.

→ **Container storage, Kwai Chung**
More than 14 million, 20ft container units moved through Hong Kong in 1997. Like LEGO toys, containers are handled by movable cranes which attach them-selves to the four corners of the box. As many as seven of these are stacked vertically, each position entirely controlled and monitored by computer and identified with a specific serial number. Private companies operate the logistics of container movement and storage.

A convincing example is the direct permutation of Kai Tak Airport to Chek Lap Kok Island. Apart from some minor teething problems, the entire move was completed overnight. This illustrates the hyper-mobility of the whole system, from its economic activities to its most specialised services.

NETWORKS, FLOWS AND TRANSITS The intersection of two roads or the shores of a pleasant riverbank used to be sufficient reason for establishing a new human settlement. Our end-of-century is characterised by the increasing scale of structures and the ever-growing network of expressways. Infrastructural nodes such as airports and motorways have become the new urban reactors. New characteristics such as fluidity and acceleration determine urban strategies such as the creation of new centres, ports or airports at some further points of the territory. Pushing this assumption further, the existing form and quality of these flows now comes into question. The original journey which only entailed a physical move from one point to another, is switched to invisible lines and patterns that move through territories, locally and globally.

Continuity, accessibility, comfort, safety and speed are the "bottom line" of the international economy. If the question of crossroads was originally related to the primacy of space, today we have switched to the primacy of time. This doesn't mean that centralities have become placeless but that they are more related to a network of high speed transportation systems, thereby making space more fluid. By extension, Fluid Machine is an ambiguous equilibrium between the hardware (machine) and the software (fluid), solid and liquid.

← **Airport Highway, Kowloon City**
Roads and highways are one of the most important network systems visible on the earth's surface. More and more complex nodes at strategic points, such as at Kai Tak Airport, are under pressure to offer more and more possible destinations. If the "spaghetti" organism was initially a nightmare for drivers, in reality it solved the problem of congestion, offering a fluid movement for vehicles.

→→ **Mobile tower quay crane, Kwai Chung**
Similar to giraffe or war machines, these tower cranes express the economic vitality of one of the most important business activities in Hong Kong. Establishing a new type of vertical landscape they are the physical link between the boat and the dockyard, the sea and the land. Around 70 of these machines cover approximately 6km of quays and are expected to handle one box every second by 2011.

→ **HK International Airport, Chek Lap Kok**
Modern travel embraces all sorts of functions other than the airport itself and those connected with air transport. Chek Lap Kok is actually a city within a city, a place of transit for travellers, but also a new town populated with service personnel. There are all kinds of 24-hour amenities such as banks, offices, hotels, restaurants, conference facilities, shopping centres in the immediate vicinity.

↑ **Modern Terminal Limited, Kwai Chung**

The question of space and efficiency was probably the first reason for private developers to build the huge Container Freight Station (CFS) and Warehouse such as Asia Terminal Centre and MTL Warehouse Building. These industrial structures provide storage and facilities for any kind of vehicle to access and transfer merchandise from the containers.

↑→→ Kai Tak Airport, Kowloon City
The long established relation between the city and the
airport was one of the highlights of a visit to Hong Kong.
Located in the midst of dense residential areas, Kai Tak
was a spectacle of proximity between buildings and
aircraft.

↑ **Container terminals, Victoria Harbour**
As the physical centre, Victoria Harbour is the place where the most intense and dynamic activities take place. Busy to the extreme, Hong Kong's waters support excessive traffic such as ferries, liners, crane barges (lighters) and container cargo. Divided into parking, roads and highways for all kinds of boats, the harbour serves to transport both men and merchandise.

↑→ Crane barge, Lamma Channel
Because of their configuration, lighters are used for mid-stream marine operations. Like insects, they attach themselves to anchor vessels, making the 62 harbour moorings very busy. Lighters are mobilised by tug boats and move around the harbour with their derricks erected.

←↑ **Storage of containers, Yuen Long**
Close to the port, airport and the border with mainland China, Yuen Long is an ideal location for the storage of empty containers. Occupying land that's yet to be developed, these container parking lots can easily be moved from one place to another. Along this "flow corridor" there is an unusual cohabitation between containers and mass-housing developments.

↑ Typhoon Shelter, West Kowloon Reclamation
Protecting boats from tropical storms, the typhoon shelter is a spectacle of machines and merchandise (containers) mixed together to form a visually chaotic scape. Indispensable to mid-stream marine operations, this is in some ways reminiscent of old Hong Kong when families used to live on their boats.

→ Reclamation site, Central
The principle of reclaiming the land to extend the territory has played an important part in Hong Kong's history. Economic acceleration, encourages the planning department to pursue this strategy in order to provide more land for construction. The process of reclaiming land, site preparation and building construction requires a large amount of energy, essentially provided by machines.

TECHNOLOGICAL UTOPIA   Mc Luhan said something along the lines of "any extension, whether skin, hand, or foot, affects the whole psychic and social complex." (2) Obviously the extension he is referring to not only concerns the physical appearance of our body but its complete nervous system.

Following the aesthetic of the machine era, human beings have been progressively displaced by computers in what is a man-machine system. With today's information network, a person can instantly communicate with the entire globe. Using the internet or mobile phones, people have returned to a nomadic condition - not a physical mobility but cerebral. At any point in time or space, we are accompanied by flows of information that's forever being updated.

As with any global centre, Hong Kong has an excessive number of mobile phones, video cameras, surveillance monitors, and digital screens. However it has developed some very specific extremes to this phenomena, using any surface to support extra layers of information. This is seen covering motorised vehicles, on walls, even at the scale of a skyscraper. Our perception directly integrates this information as a continuing intensity from the body to its immediate environment, which is ever changing. In this kind of urban   density with all its mobile data, it is impossible to escape the mediatisation of the virtual, the real advancement of electronic technologies that are submerging the entire environment.

(2) Marshall Mc Luhan. *Understanding media:
the extension of man*. NewYork: McGraw-Hill, 1964

➔   **e.bus@hk.com**
From September 1999 to April 2000 - when the tech stocks crashed - buses were covered with e.business advertising. Providing the physical reality to their virtual space, these images were transported round the entire territory to promote the new "Eldorado". This movement of information supported by moving vehicles perfectly matched the product being promoted.

↑   Airport Express, Central Station

The programme for the Airport Express railway was stated as "The new airport in Central" or the 34km distance in a 23 minute link between the Central Business District (CBD) and Chek Lap Kok Airport. An airport in the centre of the city with full check-in facilities (plus luggage) uses the same concept as its predecessor at Kai Tak. In Hong Kong, the question of proximity and accessibility is fundamental.

↑ **International Airport, Chek Lap Kok**
Part of a global city network, Hong Kong needs to provide information at all levels of international exchange. For this reason, digital screens are mounted everywhere but particularly at strategic points such as airports, stations and plazas. Displaying diverse information such as news, weather and stock exchange indices, the screens epitomise the information society.

1 23

←→ **Control room, Tsing Yi MTR Station**

The control room is for surveillance and observation. Glass boxes are either hidden or over-exposed. Linked to the outside through a series of technological instruments - video cameras, monitors, and speakers - security is their prime concern. The control room becomes the eyes and ears, receiving flows of information. Blurring the frontier between private and public domains, man and machine, its technical agents are simultaneously observers and observed by others.

RUNNING SCAPE CAN BE SCHEMATISED AS A FLAT, INFINITE TWO DIMENSIONAL SURFACE; AN UNIN-TERRUPTED PLANE WHICH IS ABLE TO EXTEND FURTHER THAN THE LIMITS OF ITS OWN SHAPE. IN HONG KONG, BOATS, CARS, CONTAINERS, TOWERS OR PEDESTRIANS ARE CONSIDERED PUNCTUATION (COMMA), MEANING THEY ARE INTEGRATED WITH THE URBAN STRUCTURE AND HAVE NO REFERENCE TO ANY PARTICULAR CENTRE (POINT). FROM THE MULTIPLE LINES OF ENERGY COMING FROM THESE ELEMENTS, A CONTINUOUS EXTENSION OF THE SYSTEM IS CREATED.

Running scape
2

"THE WHOLE SITE BEGAN TO SPEAK, ON THE WATER, ON EARTH, IN THE AIR; IT SPOKE OF ARCHITECTURE. THIS DISCOURSE WAS A POEM OF HUMAN GEOMETRY AND OF IMMENSE NATURAL FANTASY. THE EYE SAW SOMETHING, TWO THINGS: NATURE AND THE PRODUCT OF THE WORK OF MEN. THE CITY ANNOUNCED ITSELF BY THE ONLY LINE THAT CAN HARMONISE WITH THE VEHEMENT CAPRICE OF THE MOUNTAINS: THE HORIZONTAL."

Le Corbusier. *Precisions*. (1929, translation from Cambridge (Mass.): MIT Press, 1991) Pushing the image of vertical density still further, Hong Kong's landscape presents a perfect horizontal sequence shaped by three successive layers: the seashore, the building skyline and the mountain crest. The physical qualities that usually characterise islands recede when one looks towards the land from the sea. The view is of a frontal surface like a continuous urban wall.

This 360 degree visual experience provides a sensation of infinity: the observer occupies a central position and is submerged by the displayed panorama. The intensity of the spectacle is emphasised by the feeling of being both detached from and within the landscape. With this characteristic, the city exhibits itself as an effervescent illusion, a dynamic endless scene running ever faster with its economic success.

This projection creates the illusion of movement which is produced by cinematographic technique, but also the speculative investment of financial operations. Both cinema and economy offer a powerful image of the city, showing its vitality through building construction as the final materialisation of economic success.

→ **Reclamation/housing development, Hung Hom**
Reclamation plays an important role in the supply of new land. In order to maximise profits against the capital costs of developing these artificial lands, the density of mass housing is optimised.

→→ **Reclamation, Mei Fu (left), Whampoa (right)**
Both developments were built on reclaimed land and shared the privilege of being Hong Kong's highest density living environments after their completion. With further reclaimed land next door, they await another wave of private speculation.

←↑ Shenzhen from Mai Po

Along the other side of the SAR/Mainland China border is the Special Economic Zone of Shenzhen. Lack of land and non-stop speculation in Hong Kong has instigated an enormous potential for rapid urban development in the region. Shenzhen is the over-spill, receiving the excess energy from Hong Kong and spreading it throughout the Pearl River Delta.

In 1980, Shenzhen was a fishing village, now it is a metropolis of about four million inhabitants.

FLOATING LAND   63% of the world's surface is composed of oceans, seas, lakes and rivers. Therefore one has to consider the sea as another territory or potential land. Reclamation - the artificial creation of land on water, has progressively become a workable strategy for urban development. As a planning instrument, reclamation enables space to run in any direction - a sign of the former liquid condition of the land. Generally speaking, reclamation is effective in hyper-dense environments, and for this reason mainly pertains to Asian countries such as Japan, Korea, Hong Kong and Singapore. Topologically, there is a dilemma over reclaimed land in that it supersedes the original boundary between land and sea. Contentions arise such as the merging of two adverse domains - roots versus flux, solidity versus abstraction, memory versus lack of reference. A reclaimed site has no trace or inherent "quality" except in regard to its potential to extend the buildable area adjoining over-congested land. As a gigantic, free platform, reclaimed land is generally reserved for very specific "flat" programmes such as airports or container terminals (Osaka Airport, Kobe Harbour, Tokyo Bay, Seoul Airport City, Chek Lap Kok Airport, etc).

In terms of planning strategies, reclamation is an expression of the territory's economic and demographic progression, as well as the colonisation of its natural environment. From the beginning of Hong Kong's colonial history until now, successive reclamation projects have halved the original width of Victoria Harbour. The mountains fall sharply into the water as new strips of reclaimed land progressively add more vertical layers to the urban fabric. It is as if the new towers are slowly replacing the original mountainscape.

➔ **New townscape, Shatin**
Along Tolo Harbour, new towns have spread out to form a continuous ribbon of urbanisation. Developed in the early 1970s, Shatin now has a population of over half a million. Its linear extension will soon reach the latest phase of reclamation at Ma On Shan.

↑ **In-between Ma On Shan and Shatin**
The final virgin frontier between Ma On Shan, Hong Kong's most recently designated New Town, and Shatin will soon be filled with another series of private developments. The narrow strip of reclaimed land provides just enough space for a highway and one group of towers. The concept of the linear city is reduced to a minimum, a built necklace of tower blocks placed along a highspeed route.

↑ **Housing estate along the race course, Sha Tin**
The narrow width of the reclamation produces an urbanism with no articulation. Housing developments along the highway are directly connected to the race course and a new landscape is formed through the addition of lines of development that bear no relation to each other.

←→ **Reclamation site, Central**

The demand for new reclaimed land in Central Business District is a euphemism. Hong Kong has the unique potential to extend its centre, with new layers of land taken from the harbour. Subject to extensive speculation, Central's last reclamation will soon be covered with the tallest towers, adding another layer of prominence and congestion to the future skyline.

RUNNING CORRIDORS refer to the visible and invisible flows of energy that run in a linear pattern. With the growing dispersion of economic investment, the primitive concentrically planned city has evolved into a complicated territorial system, taking advantage of the emerging infrastructure of communication and transportation. These flows used be natural lines, running along river valleys or mountain axes, but are now more often artificial, inspired by the global economy. Together, they produce an alliance of multiple transportation nodes, creating linkage and articulation across geographic barriers and national borders. The configuration of this strategic network is no longer determined by local factors. The tendency is to encourage "opportunistic" development that has the capacity for global exchange, and maximises the options within each built structure. Transportation terminals are remarkable examples of the new system, whereby the function of connecting and interchanging the masses with other modes of transport is broadened to include other uses such as commercial activities, leisure facilities, offices and residential zones. These terminals also address the critical demand for various means of transportation ranging from buses, trains or planes, gigantic car parks and interchange points. Access, within this configuration becomes a measure of mobility and fluidity of urban expansion. In effect, linear developments provide the necessary dynamics for a successfully competitive centre that is able to extend its influence into the hinterlands. With no particular concern for spatial sequence or articulation, these extensive flow lines constitute an effective strategy for colonisation, transforming the landscape into a series of linear construction systems.

← HK International Airport, Chek Lap Kok
The project encompassed a new airport as well as a railway to connect the air terminal building at Chek Lap Kok with the Central Business District on Hong Kong Island. This was in addition to five highways that involved tunnels and bridges, three land reclamation projects and the construction of a new town at Tung Chung.

↑ **HK International Airport, Chek Lap Kok**
The baggage hall is an immense space inhabited by conveyor belts, digital screens and trolleys. This hall reproduces the architecture of temples where the masses used to gather for similar rituals – the difference today is that any ethnic group can perform its own unique choreography.

↑ **HK International Airport, Chek Lap Kok**
A moving walkway along a 1.5 kilometre corridor helps to steer arriving passengers towards the immigration hall. An underground subway shuttle train also accelerates departures and arrivals.

← KCR station, Kowloon Tong
Mass transportation is challenged by the magnitude of the peak hour crowds. For this reason train stations are uncommonly long and the train itself has no interior doors to separate compartments.

↑ Hong Kong Station, Central
The biggest transportation node optimises its passenger circulation through a lengthy network of corridors in order to disperse users with the maximum efficiency. The control of intense passenger traffic is possible through the accommodation of big, neutral spaces which produce a workable building with multiple inter-connected infrastructures and programmes.

CHIP-PLANNING DESCRIBES VARIOUS SPHERES OF URBAN FORMS. AN ANALYSIS OF DIFFERENT SCALES, FROM LOCAL TO GLOBAL, REVEALS THE CONTINUAL TRANSFORMATION OF THE URBAN TERRITORY. IN THE SPECIFIC CASE OF HONG KONG, A RAPID TRANSFORMATION IS MADE POSSIBLE THROUGH THE STANDARDISATION OF BUILDING, BLOCK, OR GROUP OF BLOCKS. THE OPERATION IS COMPARABLE TO THE ASSEMBLAGE OF A COMPUTER, IE. ONE MICROCHIP CAN BE REPLACED BY ANOTHER, OR THE ENTIRE SYSTEM, ITS EXTENSIONS, THE SCREEN, UNTIL THE MACHINE ITSELF IS REINVENTED IN ORDER TO BE MORE EFFICIENT.

IN THE LATE-CAPITALIST SYSTEM, ECONOMIC AND POLITICAL VOLATILITY MAKES LONG TERM PREDICTIONS IMPOSSIBLE. IN ORDER TO ANTICIPATE SUCH FLUCTUATIONS, CONSTRUCTION PROGRAMMES ALLOW FOR CONSTANT ADAPTATION: ALTERATION OF THE BLOCK, DENSIFICATION OF THE CENTRE, MULTIPLICATION OF CENTRES, EVEN THE TRANSPORTATION OF A MAJOR FUNCTION TO ANOTHER SITE.

Chip planning

3

"YES INDEED... FOR IT STRETCHES OVER THE CHANNEL AND BEYOND... INTO EUROPE. IN THIS PART YOU CAN SEE THE HABITATIONS PLUGGED INTO THE GIANT NETWORK-STRUCTURE. THIS IS 12 STOREYS HIGH AND 144 FEET LONG... WITH DIAGONALS OF LIFTS MAKING UP THE GRID... SOMETIMES RISING UP INTO UNEVEN TOWERS OF HOUSING... THE CRANE-WAY IS ALWAYS THERE SO THAT IT CAN CONTINUOUSLY BUILD AND REBUILD ITSELF. ON THE RIGHT IS A GIANT TOWER OF SERVICED FLATS FOR THE MOST MOBILE OF THE EVER-CHANGING POPULATION. THE HOVERCRAFT STATION IS IMMEDIATELY ADJOINING WITH THE STOP ON THE HIGHEST-SPEED MONORAIL... THE HOVERCRAFT ARE THEMSELVES A PART OF THE IDEA OF A EUROPEAN CITY... MOVING BUILDINGS WITH CITY FUNCTIONS SUCH AS BUSINESS DEALS AND GOVERNMENT GOING ON INSIDE... BUT WITH ALL THIS THERE DOES NOT HAVE TO BE MONOTONY..." Peter Cook - Archigram, *Plug-in City* (Drawing, 1964.) Contemporary developments in metropolitan regions result from the uncoordinated assemblage of various forces. Exposed to the instabilities of late-capitalist production, these regions have developed a polycentric structure of dense cores with competitive dispositions. Contrary to the traditional centralised city that used to correspond to one single dynamic, urban structures now spread out like a liquid and have multiple centres. Acceleration and diversification - as a weapon of international competitiveness - has also become a programme for new planning strategies. In this context, the "plug-in" method becomes effective at any scale, allowing a greater variation of urban components: a building or an entire block can easily be replaced by another; an airport or a core function substituted for a more competitive one.

➔ **Aesthetics of density, Mid-levels**
The average population density in residential areas is 2,500 persons per hectare. On the steep slopes of Mid-levels, this extreme cannot be reached, yet the highest developments are located on the upper part of the mountain. From the Peak, one can observe the world's biggest laboratory for the hyper-dense-city.

← Pencil tower, Central

New sites for 30 storey buildings often use the same footprint of a five storey one. When the next tower goes up next door, the density will be raised to the maximum.

↑ The old and the new, Mong Kok

Different eras of construction are clearly expressed by the diversity of scales and typologies. From above, the view resembles a forest of different species of vegetation. The size of the blocks and original streets have so far been preserved, making Mong Kok a work in progress where Hong Kong's history can still be read.

↑ Examples of hyper-density, Central/SheungWan
The high density of Hong Kong's skyline generates a physical atmosphere of energy and vitality. The opposite of New York's rigid planning grid, or other models of repetitive "zoning", this hectic spatial sensation perfectly illustrates what we refer to as "plug-in" planning.

↑ **Multi-use block, Central**
Located between Bank of China Tower and Hutchinson House, this block contains a parking lot on its first 10 levels. The top floor of the building is occupied by the headquarters and temporary jail of the ICAC. This kind of juxtaposition is common in Hong Kong where speculation promotes the potential to profit from any situation.

↑→ **Harbour City, Tsim Sha Tsui**

Directly connected with the ferry pier to Mainland China and Hong Kong Island is this complex of three interconnecting shopping malls: Ocean Galleries, Ocean Centre, and Ocean Terminal. First built in 1966, this building has been continuously subjected to further extensions in order to maintain its attractive situation. From the corridors of Ocean Terminal, shoppers can view the passenger liners tied up along the docks. Their appearance is fairly standard, which gives us an idea of the scale of the entire complex.

HYBRID BUT REPETITIVE Massive residential tower blocks have infiltrated Hong Kong's urban condition since the 1950's. Mass housing construction in the public sector started by using prefabricated, factory-made components for the simple reasons of construction efficiency and cost. This has created a series of standardised models that have colonised the entire territory. Recent private housing production has adopted similar typologies with a range of programmes that go far beyond the basic prototype. Each residential development forms a group of towers mounted on a podium where a highly diverse range of functional activities takes place. The residential dwelling unit or cell on offer in these complexes is more or less the same. It is the podium that becomes the major selling point, attempting to simulate paradise, and where developers sell the dreams. Like a theme park, its basic structure is covered with an embellishment of screens, walls, lights, mirrors, water and sounds. In the arena of private housing speculation, architecture is no longer the art of designing buildings, rather it provides the means to support an exclusive concept - an expression of collective fantasy. This phenomenon not only applies to residential developments but to office towers and shopping malls. Derived from such a competitive economy, their planning directly reflects the erratic demands of the market. Like the repetitive but ephemeral condition of fashion, this public core is an accumulation of a multiplicity of programmes, which is more or less the same everywhere. To be effectively competitive, a place must be plugged into an effective transportation network, propose a variety of activities, and be next to an attractive range of shopping facilities - all layered in a "beautiful" package. The appearance of the "box" is as important as its contents. Today, the growing domination of "global style" promotes a compilation of all the latest technologies (such as digital screens and high speed transportation) with decorative elements referring to both fashionable style and images of luxury.

← Apartment blocks, To Kwa Wan
In order to supply housing for an ever-increasing population, the same typology is endlessly repeated within the same area. Each block replicates the other, and is implanted at a minimum authorised distance from the others. This kind of rational building complex looks nothing like the chaotic developments that are typical of this area.

↑ **New townscape, view from Tsing Yi**
Large scale projects are individually developed wherever land is still available for construction. Together, they produce a "mixed-up-scape", with express trains and highways, vertical factories, cemeteries and the harbour. The residential high-rise bastions overlook this fantastic panorama.

→ **Residential towers, Kowloon Bay**
As there are no suburbs in Hong Kong, high density urban centres and miscellaneous facilities co-exist without any relation to each other. The ever-changing nature of these places facilitates a disparate planning model.

↑ Housing development, Kowloon reclamation

Massive residential tower blocks are mounted on a podium where a highly diverse range of activities takes place. Today's latest product, a 52 storey residential tower resembles the appearance of an urban fortress.

→ Housing development, Tuen Mun

Residential developments are usually built on prized sites. Special value is allotted to isolated yet well connected locations and this is reinforced by propaganda sales imagery of solitary blocks in the middle of rural jungle. Here the block is directly plugged into a ferry pier, forging a link with the entire territory.

←→ Private Housing development, Tung Chung
Part of the Airport Core Programme, Tung Chung new town houses a population of 160,000 within a few developments. Tung Chung Crescent is one of the biggest with 14 high rise residential towers, each 42 storeys with eight apartments per floor, and an average of five persons per apartment. With eight developments like this one, a city of 160,000 is instantly acheived.

←→ → Towers and new developments, Chai Wan and Kennedy Town

Built on totally reclaimed land, Chai Wan is the furthest east of all the urban centres on HK Island. Vertical factories and residential towers are rashly intermixed forming a brutal panorama against the surrounding landscape. On a smaller scale each visual frame contains a mountain and/or several towers.

DYNAMIC LABYRINTH REFERS TO DISORIENTATION. THIS IS REINFORCED BY THE CONSTANT CHANGES IN PLACES AND LEVELS. HONG KONG'S MAXIMUM DENSITY THRIVES ON MAXIMUM EFFICIENCY. THE RESULT IS AN ACCUMULATION OF POTENTIAL USABLE SPACES BUT ALSO AN INCREASE IN PHYSICAL MOBILITY. TO ILLUSTRATE THIS PHENOMENON, IMAGINE A KALEIDOSCOPIC ENTITY PUNCTUATED BY UNEXPECTED CHANGES AND DEVELOPING TRANSITORY SPATIAL SEQUENCES. DESPITE THE COMPLEXITY OF THIS DYNAMIC LABYRINTH, THE NEW SPATIAL ORGANISATION DELIBERATELY INDUCES THE FEELING OF SAFETY AND SECURITY, COMFORTING THE NOMADIC STROLLER TO EXPLORE FURTHER.

Dynamic Labyrinth 4

"THE FABRIC OF THE CONTEMPORARY CITY DISPLAYS AN AFFINITY WITH THE CHARAC-
TERISTICS OF RHIZOMORPHIC SYSTEMS. THE CITY IS MADE UP OF THOUSANDS OF
PLATEAUX - MATTER FORMED IN VARIOUS WAYS, WITH DIFFERENT DATA AND SPEEDS,
LINES OF ARTICULATION AND LINES OF FLIGHT... IT CONSISTS OF STRATA AND TERRITO-
RIES BUT EQUALLY INCLUDES MOVEMENTS THAT OBLITERATE STRATIFICATION AND
TERRITORIALISATION... ALL THESE LINES AND RATES OF FLOW FORM AN ASSEMBLAGE
AND AS SUCH IS UNATTRIBUTABLE... IT IS A MULTIPLICITY - BUT WE DON'T KNOW WHAT
THE MULTIPLE ENTAILS..." Gilles Deleuze, Felix Guattari, *A Thousand Plateaus*. (Paris, 1980, translation
Minneapolis: University of Minnesota Press, 1987) Floating pedestrian networks are everywhere in
Hong Kong. Detached from the street traffic, they either take the form of a pedestrian
bridge, or a labyrinth of corridors inside buildings. Whether outside or inside, open-air or
part of an air-conditioned circuit, pedestrians are able to experience a new game -
navigating the urban complexity. Before, Men used to explore new lands, now the
adventure is in recreating a world in response to new living conditions. Dynamic labyrinth
is not a sensational experiment, but results from the universal notion of an active
relationship between people and their environment, whatever forms they take. Everybody
enjoys moving from one place to another with the possibility of discovering new shops
and facilities. Spatial mobility and continuous human migration create a kaleidoscopic
motion, providing these artificial lands with a prime functional space between the
apartment and the urban territory.

→ **Pedestrian bridge, Central**
From above, the floating network appears as a three-
dimensional pedestrian space with connections to every
building. This system is designed for maximum flexibility and compatibility with the extensive density planned
for the CBD.

THE FLOATING WAY   The rapid, non-stop changes of rhythms, the variations between exterior and interior, and the link between public and private constitute a unique urban profile that's difficult to map. Numerous circulation levels and the layering of multiple programmes (uses) add even more confusion. Generally the network of mobility consists of flows, concentrations of people moving towards specific lines or points. In a study of pedestrian movements during the 1970s the Situationist Group developed the Theory of Drifting (2). They observed that "the factor of chance [with respect to people's movements] is less important than we can imagine: from the drifting angle, cities show a psycho-geographic shape, with constant streams, fixed points, and turbulence which makes access to or exit from certain zones, very difficult."

The Situationist's theory of "drifting" can be applied to Hong Kong, which is already organised by a dynamic system. Analysing historical maps of Central over the last 10 years shows that the pedestrian walkway network represents the only stable element of the system. As opposed to the buildings that surround it, access to the bridge network is left unchanged. Renamed "Floating Way" by Japanese researchers (3), the elevated pedestrian network constitutes the vertical expansion of Central's overcrowded environment. It provides an alternative route, which is distinct from that at ground level. In effect, the complete network allows a safe and quick circuit devoid of vehicle circulation and stops at road intersections.

(2) Guy-Ernest Debord, "Theorie de la derive" in, *International Situationiste*. Paris: Fayard, 1997
(3) See *Space Design*. No 330, March 1992

← Pedestrian deck, Central
Running above the congested traffic, Central's pedestrian networks are the fastest route from the ferry piers to the skyscrapers, from the Escalator to the shopping malls, or at the very least from one building to another.

↑→ Interior streets, Tseung Kwan O

Interior streets create an artificial environment totally oriented towards shopping. The street is a linear space lined with continuous shop windows displaying all kinds of new products. Each window competes with the others for maximum diversity, the brightest colours and attractive prices. The linearity is emphasised by low ceilings and smooth surfaces with uniform reflective marble or tiled floors. Centres in new towns have developed a non-stop commercial-scape, and even the pedestrian bridges are inhabited by an uninterrupted sequence of shops between the malls.

→→ Interchange platform, Lam Tim

Occupying the basement of a multi-programmed complex, this interchange platform is a dark, noisy and highly polluted public space. Vehicular traffic on the highway crosses two floating pedestrian walkways, giving the tunnel a sense of contradictory scales. Along the highway and connected to the footbridges, an open pedestrian path branches off to buses and other motorised transportation.

A LIQUID JOURNEY "The Escalator's path coincides with what was people's most favoured walking route up the hillside, prior to its existence. As a result, it is not a straight line engraved concurrently with the slope, but rather a split inscribed in the topography. Its curves and breaks remind us that its trajectory was pre-existing at the original ground level and preferred to other possibilities. Moreover, because it channels people in one line, it has drawn out the most logically flexible course. The Escalator can be read like a vector, a directional space. In that sense it is not two points which define the line of its trajectory. On the contrary, the trajectory defines the starting point that allows it to exist.

The numerous stops, as well as entrances and exits inscribe the intervals, which give rhythm to the duration of the journey. As an open space, the Escalator wraps both destination and destiny in the same way. Contrary to the anarchic movement of a crowd in the street, those on the walkway are ordered and specifically regulated. The individual is dissolved in the impersonalised flux of the masses. It is through this furtive contact that people and things appear and disappear in a continuous flow. Continuity only exists in this vertiginous relationship linked with mechanical motion. Through its dynamic the Escalator is a vectorial image that travels from one segment to another and from where the city appears and disappears according to its crossed layers. Along its way, it opens and closes on ordinary scenes of daily life, which are played successively by the same actors and spectators."(4)

(4) Extract from: gutierrez + portefaix,
"A Liquid Journey" in *hinge*, vol.54, 1998

→ **Central - Mid-levels escalator, Central**
Like a river, the moving walkway flows as a one way stream. Nevertheless, its direction varies depending on the demands of the greatest number of users. Every morning from 6am to 10am, the moving walkway projects the masses down towards the commuting intersections and the CBD.

← Central - Mid-levels escalator, Central

As a new element in the urban context, the escalator cuts through the density, interrupting the pre-existing order. Like a tributary, it controls and organises the landscape along its route: sometimes it becomes a large river, sometimes a narrow bottleneck. Its proximity to the windows of adjacent buildings produces an enigmatic in-between space.

↑ Shark aquarium, Ocean Park

The shark and ray aquarium has a transparent tunnel underneath where visitors can observe the fish as if from the sea floor. A slow moving walkway leads them from the entrance to the exit of the tunnel, enabling the user to fully concentrate on the unusual spectacle.

←→ Central - Mid-levels escalator, Central

From above, the escalator resembles entrails twisting through the urban fabric. The structure of the whole is elementary. It is an assemblage of standard elements made of steel tubes that support a translucent plastic cover. The latter is a specific architectonic element, visible from inside to outside, and has a direct function: to shelter. Its vaulted form is a unifying element of the whole.

← Hongkong and Shanghai Bank, Central

Instead of the typical plaza in front of prestigious buildings, the Bank offers an open space in its basement. A pair of escalators, which run up through a glazed veil, connects this plaza to the main banking hall. Transparency and diagonal movement, emphasised by the 10 storey atrium give the bank its unique magnetic character.

↑ Festival Walk, Kowloon Tong

The largest shopping mall in Hong Kong, its planning was developed with the minimum of connections between floors. This strategy obliges consumers to walk the length of all the shops ensuring that any location within the plan is profitable.

VERTICAL ASSEMBLAGE   Verticalisation - meaning a vertical assemblage of programmes and forms - is an important way of maintaining maximum freedom of usage
within a   building. In other words, "it is the instrument of a new form of unknowable
urbanism" (5). This potential absolutely suits Hong Kong's development as it allows a
building to compete in order to attract the most prestigious occupants. For example when
a new skyscraper is launched, the challenge to buy or rent space in it subsequently
involves other buildings, pulling them into a game of move out /move in tag. Occupation
of space varies both with economic fluctuation and even fashion - when an influential
occupant decides to move, others immediately follow suit.

Vertical assemblage also allows an arbitrary programme of uses within a building. A
famous example is Chungking Mansions (6) - a four level podium supporting five blocks,
each 17 storeys and accommodating: 188 private apartments, 82 hostels, dormitories or
guest- houses, 56 factories or offices, 18 restaurants, plus a few unknown and locked
places. In addition to its permanent occupants - more than 20 resident nationalities
representing various religions, and a large number of "unidentified" tourists ceaselessly
dominate the majority of its space(s), developing a type of edge city within a single
building.

(5) Rem Koolhaas. *Delirious New York*.
New York: Monacelli Press, 1978
(6) Forthcoming book, gutierrez + portefaix. *HK story n°4,*
Chungking Mansions. Hong Kong: map book, 2001

4 21

→   **Pacific Place, Admiralty**
The atrium reveals a vertical accumulation of disparate
activities. The cafe creeps under the internal street,
using fake decor and lighting to recreate an intimate
atmosphere similar to a Parisian coffee shop.

↑→ 5th, 7th, 11th, 13th floors, Causeway Bay

As it ascends, the elevator lift establishes a direct
relationship with the multiple programmes along its
route. With a total absence of articulation, each stop is
a gate into a different scenario: a restaurant, a game
centre, a karaoke box, a nightclub, a gymnasium, etc.
The building is a stack of individual premises, and
allows a continuous change of use and programme.

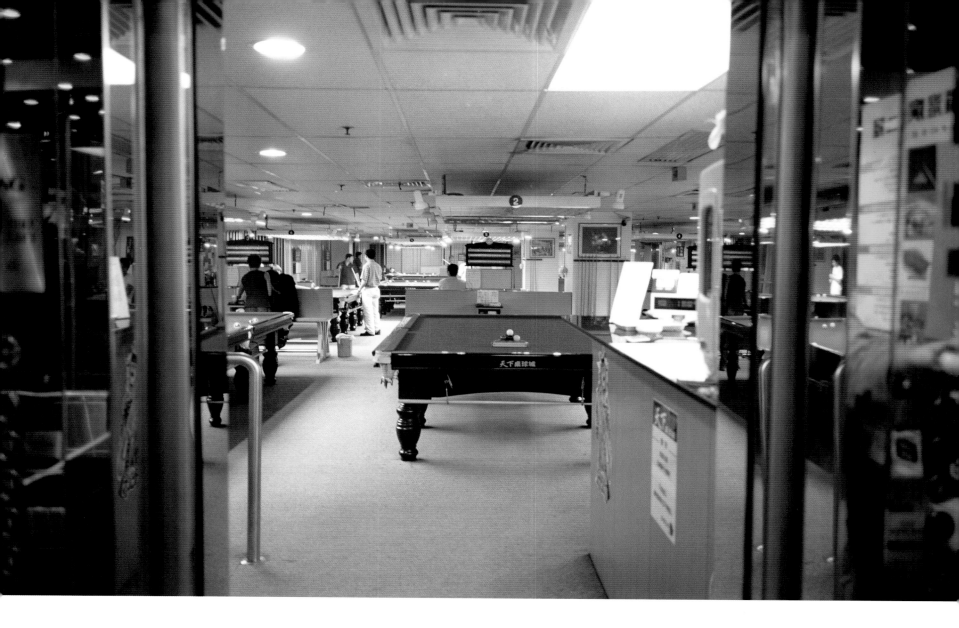

APPROPRIATED PLACE IS A NEW TYPE OF DOMAIN. THE TRADITIONAL DICHOTOMY OF PUBLIC VERSUS PRIVATE SPACE NO LONGER EXISTS IN HONG KONG'S NEW URBAN CONTEXT. INSTEAD OF THIS DUALITY, THERE IS THE TRANSITION ZONE, A SPACE THAT LIES BETWEEN ONE'S OWN PRIVATE INDIVIDUAL BODY AND THE PUBLI-CITY SYSTEM. THESE SPACES ARE DELIMITED BY MOVEMENT AND EXCHANGE: SHOPPING MALLS, AS MASS MAGNETS, BECOME THE PARADIGM OF A NEW SOCIETY, WHERE THE NOMADIC CONSUMER LOSES HIS INDIVIDUALITY TO BECOME JUST ANOTHER PRODUCT OF THE ECONOMIC SYSTEM. IN THE DESERT, THE OASIS IS AN ILLUSTRATIVE PLACE WHERE EVERYBODY CAN "WATER THEIR FLOCK"; IT IS NOT A PRIVATE OR A PUBLIC SPACE, BUT AN APPROPRIATED PLACE.

Appropriated place 5 111

"PUBLIC SPACE IS MADE AND NOT BORN. A PUBLIC SPACE IN A CITY IS PRODUCED BY A GOVERNMENT AGENCY (IN THE FORM OF A PARK) OR BY A PRIVATE CORPORATION (IN THE FORM OF A PLAZA IN FRONT OF AN OFFICE BUILDING, OR AN ATRIUM INSIDE THE BUILDING). WHAT'S PRODUCED IS A PRODUCT: IT'S BARTERED BY THE CORPORATION IN EXCHANGE FOR AIR RIGHTS, FOR THE RIGHT TO BUILD THEIR BUILDING HIGHER, IT'S GRANTED BY THE GOVERNMENT AGENCY, TO PEOPLE AS A PUBLIC BENEFIT, AS PART OF A WELFARE SYSTEM." Vito Acconci. *Making Public.* (La Haye: Stroom Hcbk, 1993) Hong Kong is a hyper-dense market city. The streets are subject to a non-stop flow of people who daily transit from home to work. Outside peak hours, the crowds still occupy the numerous shopping destinations dispersed throughout the urban territory. In this context, public space is an amenity that exists beyond commercial activities. It frequently inhabits the spaces in-between two buildings or two streets, but is definitely outside the bounds of speculation. Viewed from above, public spaces appear as a series of holes cutting the density, but from the street they are almost invisible unless you venture into the narrow paths between the blocks.

In effect, these open spaces serve a primary role - as an extension to the over-congested residential apartments. Within the old street patterns of Wanchai, Sai Ying Pun or Mong Kok, the youth and the elderly overcome this congestion by occupying playgrounds and gardens. Their relative closeness to the apartment and the number of facilities offered, create opportunities for neighbourhood community life. Everyone knows what everyone else is doing: running or sitting, playing badminton or mahjong, chatting or listening to the domestic birds in their cages hung on trees.

← **SOGO corner, Causeway Bay**
This strategic intersection is like a battlefield - crowds of pedestrians fighting against heavy traffic. In alternate sequence, each is determined to follow their respective routes. This battle is generally solved by the construction of an overhead pedestrian bridge that separates the two competing circulation systems. This is a rare example of equity between pedestrians and vehicles.

↑ Public holes in Mong Kok
Viewed from above, street level public places appear as parking lots. Furthermore, both involve similar regulations. For example, one has the right to take a place if it is empty and can keep it - provided you don't move. These public holes, whether temporary or permanent, create an opportunity to cut the hyper-density with emptiness or greenery.

→ Basketball arena, Wanchai
Public space includes sports fields open 24 hours a day, seven days a week. Observed from the streets, sports activities add another dynamic to the continuous running movements of the masses. At night, the playing field is turned into a sea of light floating between the buildings and the street.

PLAZA AND ATRIUM   With recent building developments, former public spaces have been replaced by different types of spaces that are no longer public but appropriated. The expansion of hermetically sealed environments controlled with electric lights, video surveillance and air-conditioning, these free pockets are directly absorbed within the enclosed built mass of the podium or in the shopping centre. The dominant podium model has become the new domain between the private flat and the city, while shopping centres have progressively created an attractive internal network between the office and the public transportation system. The shopping centre organised inside the podium is a third option to combine the two programmes within the same envelope.

An appropriated place officially belongs to a private corporation. It therefore obviously requires an interdisciplinary marketing strategy so the product can compete successfully, whether residential or commercial. These spaces are allowed to be appropriated by city users - those who inhabit the city and contribute to the economic system. With spatial control and private building management operations, appropriated places are completely secure, but this is in exchange for the presence of commercial activities. Furthermore this deal ensures that there's no violence, homelessness, or drugs, so with no interference users are immediately transformed into potential consumers. Inside the perfect haven of the synthetic environment, people feel protected and "at home". The plaza and atrium are private spaces disguised as public ones. In this sense, they are largely responsible for the increasingly blurred spatial relationship between public and private domains. Whether located outside or inside the building, they generally appear as a transition between different scales or functions. First, they exist as emptiness, as a "negative" against the surrounding highly concentrated construction. Second, they represent the public face of the building or group of buildings, and so must have a perfectly controlled image. Third, it is this component that competes most aggressively in the market.

➜ Grand Millennium Plaza, Sheung Wan
Exploiting the concept of a European piazza, Grand Millennium Plaza uses the natural changes in ground level for a succession of baroque stairs, bronze fountains, granite paving and palm trees. The environment is completely private though it looks like a natural aperture cutting through the density. However the heavy presence of security agents and an evident lack of seating make it a place to cross, rather than to rest.

← Landmark Atrium, Central

Dazzling shopping malls and their atriums, extravagant hotel lobbies, and generous banking halls are designed to seduce consumers. In Central, every building is dressed for the elite consumer society.

↑ Sunshine City, Ma On Shan

With its glazed open roof, this brand new commercial space functions as a covered public plaza. Fake stone bridges, fountains and *candelabras*, divide the space into multiple alleys leading to various shopping circuits. The "generous" atmosphere is reinforced by the aggregation of decorative elements, excessively over-filling this popular private domain.

SHOPPING   Today's shopping, in terms of its influence on the urban environment, is deliberately stronger than ever before. This effect is evident both in gigantic shopping malls - the new temples of consumption - and in the streets where pedestrian lanes attract all kinds of mobile shops. The former is a permanent urban centre drawing the crowds through its gigantic spaces, while the latter is residual and caters to everyday needs. Together, they form a complete network where one cannot escape from shopping. New shopping marketing strategies have infiltrated every specific programme of the city. In the airport, taking a plane has almost become a secondary function. Chek Lap Kok is an effective model for retail opportunity: shopping points and arcades accompany passengers from the check-in counters, to the departure lounge, and to their seat on the aircraft - and vice versa. Numerous global and local brands are organised so that there is a small sample of all the merchandise. Similarly, transportation stations are planned along a strategic commercial channel, with the addition of bigger pockets formed by mall complexes, hotels, stadiums, universities, etc. This hybrid combination of building programmes has produced a reality, which is invariably turned towards one single goal: shopping.

In addition, new retail marketing technologies actively participate in the celebration. Designers and architects have found a boundless market to produce attractive place creating a positive battlefield where each retailer has to stand apart from the others. Consumption, as a liberating form of unpredictability and freedom has found an elected area to consolidate its new reign.

→ **City'super, Causeway Bay**
The City'super retail store possesses a circular travelator which is unique to Hong Kong. As with New York's Guggenheim Museum, the strategy is to stretch the distance and therefore the length of time people spend in the venue. Moving around the central atrium, consumers are totally submerged in the displayed merchandise.

→ → **Times Square, Causeway Bay and Pacific Place, Admiralty**

Plaza and atrium are used for promotional events and exhibitions, completely filling the supposedly open spaces. Plasma screens and special lighting and sounds contribute to create an atmosphere totally dedicated to advertising and shopping.

← MTR Station, Causeway Bay

Advertising has invaded every empty area of the subway, so that any potential surface becomes a hypersurface. Recent market strategies mean that expensive marbles or fancy steel panels are no longer necessary. The material aspect of the interior disappears leaving images attached to floors, columns, walls, ceilings, etc.

↑ MTR, Central

In addition to the recent wrapping of buses, train coaches present a dynamic system of advertising. Every mode of transport transcends its original function of moving people to become information in motion. An accumulation of layers - from the exterior walls to the interior surfaces of the train compartment and the light-boxes outside, produces the sensation of being completely surrounded.

← ← Prostitution lightscape, Mong Kok
Sex is one product that is not exhibited in shop windows. In Hong Kong prostitution is signalled by yellow light-boxes and rows of red and blue neon. These differ from other commercial signs because of their strict adherence to colour codes and the arrow shaped neon.

←→ Neon signs, Causeway Bay & Tsim Sha Tsui
Neon signs hanging on the built facades draw the architecture and urbanscape into the dominant commercial language of culture. Appropriating the empty space over the street, they transform the urban scene into a three dimensional marketplace. Symbols and brand names dominate the environment.

GLOBAL STYLE, LOCAL TRADE   Hong Kong is an over-exposed supermarket.

Strategically, it is the place where the global economy and local market confront each other, forming an expansive battlefield throughout the territory. The dominant forces of globalisation are weakened by powerful Chinese commercial operations that control the world's biggest factory. Like anywhere else, Hong Kong gently absorbs Italian, Parisian and Japanese fashions. However, 10 times that volume is simultaneously produced and sold on the streets as cheap copies. So when a new product is introduced to the market, whether it is clothes, a watch or a VCD, it is instantly reproduced and diffused at one tenth of its price everywhere.

Street trading has been a feature of life in Hong Kong for over a hundred years. Whether fixed to one location or itinerant, hawkers still prosper alongside the modern capitalist megaliths. After years of trying to disperse these humble activities to peripheral urban locations, planners have now realised the tourist potential of hawker markets and encouraged their return to central neighbourhoods. As a result, and contrary to many other global cities, the Central Business District has to endure the persistent assault of "illegal" merchandise; fakes which flourish a few metres from the Gucci, Burberrys or Christian Dior shops. In Hong Kong's case, street hawkers have developed a powerful local network of "Chinese labelled" products. While international capitalism promotes western fashions and Japanese technologies, the local market responds with immediate adoption and hyper-diffusion. The itinerant shops on wheels actively participate in spreading hawker's wares around the city, inducing the consumer to buy immediately as the next day they may be at another location. This frenetic rhythm of consumption and continuous turnover of products emphasises their ephemeral condition - a cult of desire or a prescription against boredom.

→ **Itinerant or permanent street hawkers, Central**
With lack of space and in such extreme densities, Hong Kong is always developing new strategies to reinvent shopping. Shop units can be as deep as 30cm with products displayed in rows, or strange boats on wheels, which disappear as fast as they appear. As a consequence, shopping infiltrates all kinds of spaces, everywhere.

↑ **Circulation and distribution, Sheung Wan**
To maximise product sales in such minimum space without any back-up or storage requires an efficient system of circulation and distribution. Every Saturday, hundreds of lorries supply the dry fish market in Sheung Wan. The merchandise is delivered while consumers gather to get the best choice. The result is that both the streets and the pedestrian spaces are paralysed by the frenetic exchanges.

← **Street market, Central**

Found all over Hong Kong street markets are a succession of open-air portable shops forming a row in front of the permanent shops at ground level. Usually arranged in two parallel rows occupying the wider aspect of the street, they segregate the former public space into three narrow lanes. The flow of people fuses with the flow of food, clothing, and electronic gadgets, making the street market one of the busiest place in Hong Kong.

← **Hongkong and Shanghai Bank, Central**

On Sundays and public holidays, Hong Kong's Central District is occupied by thousands of Filipino girls who transform the public space around the empty office towers into a collective living room. A cartographic image of the places they use presents a clear picture of public and private space in Central. They occupy Statue Square and Chater Garden, either side of the Legislative Council Building. They are authorised to sit, picnic or dance in Chater Road, which is closed to vehicle circulation on these occasions. They can also use the public elevated walkways – both on and underneath. Although they are permitted to conduct purchases in the commercial centres and use the pedestrian bridge systems, they cannot linger there. One exception is the open ground floor of the Hongkong and Shanghai Bank that is made public by the Filipinos on their days off.

↑ **Home with no walls, Sheung Wan**

Along highways, building sites and in Hong Kong's industrial areas, there are people who use public spaces as their home. This form of occupation is not made with cardboard or cloth, yet it is a home - with kitchen, living room and bedroom – but no walls. Here the privacy of the body is put on public view.

SOFT DISAPPEARANCE DEFINES THE BRIEF MOMENT BETWEEN DEMOLITION AND REDEVELOPMENT, WHEN URBAN FRAGMENTS ARE VISIBLE LIKE RUINS. FOR INSTANCE DURING THE TRANSITION PERIOD BEFORE A NEW STRUCTURE EMERGES, THE EMPTIED LAND IS NOT GIVEN A CHANCE TO ABSORB ANY LAYERS OF HISTORY, BUT IS TURNED INTO A CARPARK FOR A FEW WEEKS.

LIKE A LIVING ORGANISM, HONG KONG DISPOSES OF ITS UNADAPTED CELLS AND REPLACES THEM WITH MORE ADAPTED OR COMPETITIVE ONES. THIS KIND OF MUTATION, OR POLITICAL PERMUTATION, CHANGES THE IMAGE OF THE CITY BUT NEVER ITS IDENTITY.

HONG KONG IS BY DEFINITION A PLACE OF TRANSITION.

Soft disappearance 6

6 03

"FROM THE AESTHETICS OF THE APPEARANCE OF A STABLE IMAGE - PRESENT AS AN ASPECT OF ITS STATIC NATURE - TO THE AESTHETICS OF THE DISAPPEARANCE OF AN UNSTABLE IMAGE - PRESENT IN ITS CINEMATOGRAPHIC FLIGHT OF ESCAPE - WE HAVE WITNESSED A TRANSMUTATION OF REPRESENTATIONS. THE EMERGENCE OF FORMS AS VOLUMES DESTINED TO PERSIST AS LONG AS THEIR MATERIALS WOULD ALLOW HAS GIVEN WAY TO IMAGES WHOSE DURATION IS PURELY RETINAL." Paul Virilio, "The Overexposed City" (in *Lost Dimension*. New York: Semoitext(e), 1991) In Hong Kong, there is as much destruction as construction. The continuous alternation between these two states - the old and the new - has shaped the skyline like the blurred image where the mountains melt, the sea evaporates, and new buildings emerge directly from the ruins of their predecessors. Disappearance is not a matter of effacement but rather replacement and substitution. Considering the territory as a stratification of various layers over time, it appears that its fragments form concurrently, as a heterogeneous entity. Hong Kong is a place where alternation is natural and therefore supposes a high degree of absorption and adaptation. Focusing on urban phenomena, the notion of soft disappearance introduces another aspect of cartography with different parameters. Recognising these limits necessitates a knowledge of all the multiple lines of demarcation spread across the territory, and identifying each of these enclaves as a singular domain. It means charting undiscovered fields in order to render them visible. Ackbar Abbas (2) wrote, "any description then that tries to capture the features of the city will have to be, to some extent at least, stretched between fact and fiction [...] A spatial history of disappearance will attempt to evoke the city rather than claim to represent it, in the sense of giving a definitive account of what it is really like."

← Old Chinese village, Pak Sha O
This traditional Hakka village is a rare left behind from Hong Kong's effervescent activities. Protected by an enclosed valley and far enough from the road, this preserved part of the New Territories is home to an extraordinary variety of flora and fauna.

(2) Ackbar Abbas. *Hong Kong - Culture and the Politics of Disappearance*. Minneapolis: University of Minnesota Press, 1997

↑ **Mountain scape, Lamma Island**
The mountains are a metaphor of the ever-changing character of the territory. Hong Kong's geography is both a powerful and unstable element.

→ **Bird reservoir, Mai Po**
In between the urban densities of Shenzhen and Yuen Long, Mai Po is an important area of untouched natural habitat of ecological value. With the recent urbanisation of the New Territories, this remote piece of land has become a rarity in the region. As a protected area, it also has a poignant strategic role, denoting the boundary between Mainland China and the SAR.

←→ Tsang Tai Uk Walled Village, Sha Tin
In many parts of the New Territories, walled villages are interspersed with new developments. The few remaining examples (this one dates from 1850) are still occupied by some traditional clans (usually the eldest) who own it. These villages are becoming a valuable tourist asset, particularly in the eyes of foreigners.

↑ **Old shop, Central**

Traditional commerce successfully resists the propagation of supermarkets and multinational product chains. Street markets and shops specialising in Chinese food, such as dried fish or eggs remain standing despite their deteriorated condition.

↑ Old building, Sai Ying Pun

In Western district, typical low-rise old buildings are mixed with high-rise residential towers. People still live in these buildings despite their fragile condition, and will probably stay until they are replaced by new high rise construction.

URBAN ENTROPY   All architecture dreams of escaping its entropic conclusion. Entropy refers to the non-stop contraction of energy within a system; a reduction defined by the growing disorder of its internal material. By definition, entropy is a negative movement: firstly it infers order, and finally the irreversible destruction of that order. This can happen in various ways - through defacement or redundancy, but in Hong Kong's context it is particularly manifested as accumulation and profusion. This was the case with the late Kowloon Walled City where destruction was the ultimate phase of its entropic trajectory. The articulation of multiplicity and complexity in some of Hong Kong's urban structures displays a great richness in terms of living density. For example, Diamond Hill village is impressive because of its perpetual potential to transform and adapt to the reality of people's lives. Its inhabitants have demonstrated that hyper-density can create acceptable spaces, with sufficient public space to create a lively community. Made of cheap materials, often salvaged from demolition sites, each house offers the minimum space necessary for everyday life. Each layer or extension to the original structure is built on top of its parent, hence preserving its history like the pages of a book. In general, Hong Kong's economic/political solutions only allow for the singular and systematic *tabula rasa* of an entire area, which is then offered up as an object of speculation, multiplying its vertical density by 10 times.

→   →→   **Traditional village, Diamond Hill**
Construction work proceeds at a drastic rate everywhere. There are few pockets that have escaped the demolition-construction process. However, Diamond Hill is an extraordinary model of self-made construction. Hidden beneath the chaos is a complex organisation of street markets, public places, gardens, and interior patios that puncture the extreme density.

↑→ Three street types, Diamond Hill
Buildings are typically two storey and constructed of
steel and wood. Shops opening onto the commercial
streets or entrances leading into a mini-courtyard,
occupy the ground floors, while the upper levels are
used for living quarters and bedrooms.

↑ **Moored boats, Causeway Bay typhoon shelter**
Dwellings on the water have become a rarity. Popularised in films, a limited number of traditional sampans remain today. In the shelter, moored craft are a mixture of two extremes: expensive yachts owned by members of the Royal Hong Kong Yacht Club, and small wooden sampans where a few old Chinese residents still live.

← **Pui Man village, Kowloon City**

Hidden behind the recent developments, traces of the old urban fabric have escaped wholesale *tabula rasa*. These buildings may not meet minimum standards, yet they support a strong sense of community with generous public spaces alongside the narrow houses. Made with an infinity of eclectic materials, these houses are a exceptional example of self-made habitats.

URBAN INTERSTICES   Urban void, or in French *terrain vague*, is a measure of the territory's future potential. Mapping the presence of these voids is another way of interpreting Hong Kong's urban phenomena, especially its major transformations. A definition of *vague* implies something undefined, ambiguous, imprecise, ie. that is not yet possible to qualify, which has no identified limits or distinct functions. These wastelands could be transformed into productive extensions of the existing urban fabric, and either opened to speculation or used for public space. Voids are an important part of the contemporary landscape. Paradoxically, their presence is revealed by absence, ie. a negative of the built density and thus they have a special meaning. Therefore, they must be preserved or constantly replaced in alternation with other new ones.

There are plenty of abandoned areas in major world cities but lack of land in Hong Kong makes these rare interstices of very special value. However, despite continuous expansion, many parts of the territory still possess enormous potential for construction. One reason has been the displacement of major industrial activities to the Pearl River Delta region, which has created opportunities for land conversion. A similar precedent is the Kai Tak Airport site (270 hectares) which has been left empty for about three years. Another explanation could be that the cycle of destruction/construction is more intense here than anywhere else, particularly when compared with a historical city. Cleared sites exist in large quantities, even if for a very short period of time. Finally, the urgent quest for land obliges the government to instigate long term and large scale visions. Mammoth projects need to be planned well in advance so there are always areas of cleared or reclaimed land lying in wait for future development. However because their destiny is marked for development, these "temporary" spaces must be maintained or substituted by others in order to preserve the level of contingency demanded by the system.

← Hyper-density, North Point
With this typical image of an organic block, it is difficult to say if it is one entity or a multiplicity of fragments stacked together. Illegal extensions on facades and roofs make progressive links from one building to the next, binding the whole block towards the same destiny.

← Foundation weight, Sheung Wan
Slender towers require very deep foundations to enable maximum height. Piled into the ground with archaic machines, the steel bars are like the invisible part of an iceberg. Once this first stage is completed, mountains of concrete blocks are placed over the ground during the following weeks to test the resistance of the new foundations.

↑ Kowloon Walled City monument, Kowloon
Some considered it a living monster, others a fantastic example of organic, self-made architecture. Whatever point of view, it has left a distinguished mark on HK. When it was finally razed a few years ago, a monument was erected in its place at the centre of a park. Aside from the dark side of its previous existence, the preservation of the ruins from the KWC tells an embellished story of what was a unique architectural example.

↑ Destruction site, Sheung Wan
When a building is destroyed there is no violent explosion or instant collapse. The process involves wrapping
the building in a special resistant material, after which
it is attacked from top to bottom by an army of hammer
drills. During the following months, the original volume
slowly melts until it completely disappears.

→ End of destruction, Sheung Wan
A ruined camp is an obligatory stage between the old
and the new. During this period, neighbourhood life is
interrupted, in anticipation of the next resident. There
is little recycling (unlike Mainland China), and no trace
of the previous building will be visible after the new
one is erected.

↑→ New housing development, Tseung Kwan O
New 52 storey developments involve a mixture of construction techniques using both bamboo scaffolding and cranes. Wrapped in green netting until the facades are finished, these massive structures are planted in the landscape like curious creatures with no scale. For a second this could be a dinosaur, a fortress or perhaps Albi Cathedral...

Acknowledgements

First of all, we are grateful to Anna Koor who was challenged by this editing. For years she has generously supported our writings, giving us the opportunity to make it intelligible and publishable. We extend our gratitude to Ackbar Abbas for his invaluable criticism and encouragement with the conception and production of this book. We also thank Norman Jackson Ford and Nick Koor, for their careful readings.

Christophe Barthelemy and Pamela Kember have contributed to the book through their critical interventions in the text and their continuous moral support. Raymond Chan stimulated our first steps. We extend our thanks to the M.arch students of the Department of Architecture at The Chinese University of Hong Kong, who during a period between 1996 and 1999 produced a very exciting reading of Hong Kong for their studio projects. Steven Haughton opened our eyes to some of his secret places.

We thank Gerard Henry at the Alliance Française for believing in the project.

Nora Amrouni and Edgar Gonsalvez helped with the graphic conception and supported our transgressions. Benoit Dupuis and Morgan Ommer gave us precious advice.

Some special thanks are due to Caroline Barat, Karim Davezak, Thomas Dubuisson, Anne-Celine Jean and Nathalie Mangharam, for their support and friendship.

We finally express our gratitude to our friend Cyrille Hanappe from whom we received our first invitation to Hong Kong five years ago.

References

- Ackbar ABBAS, *Hong Kong - Culture and the Politics of Disappearence*. Minneapolis: University of Minnesota Press, 1997.

- Vito ACCONCI, *Making public*. The Hague: Uitgever, 1993.

- Louis ARAGON, *Le paysan de Paris*. Paris: Gallimard, 1926.

- Anna ARENDT, *Condition de l'homme moderne*. Paris: Calmann-Levy, 1990.

- François ASCHER, *Metapolis ou l'avenir des villes*. Paris: O.Jacob, 1995.

- Marc AUGÉ, *Non-lieux*. Paris: Seuil, 1992.

- Reyner BANHAM, *Los Angeles - The Architecture of Four Ecologies*. London: Penguin Books, 1971.

- Guusje BENDELER, Leontine van den BOOM, Mart HULSPAS, *Nat & Droog*. Rijkswaterstaat: Architectura & Natura, 1998.

- Walter BENJAMIN, *Das Passagen-Werk*. Frankfurt am Main: Suhrkamp Verlag, 1982.

- Walter BENJAMIN, *L'homme, le langage et la culture*. Paris: Denoël-Gonthier, 1971.

- Fernand BRAUDEL, *La Méditerranée*. Paris: Flammarion, 1985.

- Jorge Luis BORGES. *Ficciones*. Buenos Aires: Emerce Editores, 1956.

- Susan BUCK-MORSS. *The dialectics of seeing*. Cambridge (Mass.): MIT Press, 1991.

- Massimo CACCIARI. *Architecture and Nihilim: On the Philosophy of Modern Architecture*. New Haven: Yale UP, 1993.

- Italo CALVINO. *Le citta invisibili*. Torino: Giulio Einaudi Editore, 1972.

- Manuel CASTELLS, *The rise of the Network Society*. Oxford: Blackwell Publishers, 1996.

- Manuel CASTELLS, *End of Millennium*. Oxford: Blackwell Publishers, 1998.

- COLLECTIVE, *Documenta X*. Ostfildern-Ruit: Cantz, 1997.

- COLLECTIVE, *Reflections On and By Marshall Mc Luhan*. Cambridge (Mass.): MIT Press, 1996.

- COLLECTIVE, *Eating Brazil*. Rotterdam: 010 Publishers, 1999.

- CONTANT, *New Babylon*. Paris: Cercle d'Art, 1997.

- Michel De CERTEAU, *L'invention du quotidien*. Paris: Gallimard, 1990.

- Hubert DAMISH, *Ruptures, Cultures*. Paris: Ed. de Minuit, 1976.

- Hubert DAMISH, *Skyline*. Paris: Seuil, 1996.

- Mike DAVIS, *City of Quartz*. London: Verso, 1990.

- Guy DEBORD, *La société du spectacle*. Paris: Gallimard, 1992.

- Luc DELEU, *The unadapted City*. Rotterdam: Nai Publishers, 1996.

- Gilles DELEUZE, Felix GUATTARI, *Mille Plateaux - Capitalisme et schizophrénie*. Paris: Les Editions de Minuit, 1980.

- Michel FOUCAULT, *Les mots et les choses*. Paris: Gallimard, 1966.

- Anthony GAR-ON YEH, *Planning Hong Kong For The 21 st Century*. Hong Kong: C.U.P.E.M. University of Hong Kong, 1996.

- Greg GIRARD, Ian LAMBOT, *City of darkness*. Hong Kong: Watermark, 1993.

- Dan GRAHAM, *Rock my religion*. Dijon: Les Presses du Reel, 1993.

- Jürgen HABERMAS, *Le discours philosophique de la modernité*. Paris: Gallimard, 1988.

- Franz HESSEL, *Promenade dans Berlin*. Grenoble: PUF Grenoble, 1989.

- Rem KOOLHAAS, *New York Délire*. Paris: Chêne, 1978.

- Siegfried KRACAUER, *Rues de Berlin et d'ailleurs*. Paris: Ed. du Promeneur, 1994.

- Siegfried KRACAUER, *Jacques Offenbah ou le secret du Second Empire*. (1937) Paris: Ed. du Promeneur, 1994.

- Henri LEFEBVRE, *Le droit à la ville*. Paris: Anthropos, 1968.

- Marshall MC LUHAN. *Understanding media: the extension of man*. New York: McGraw-Hill, 1964.

- MVRDV. *FARMAX*. Rotterdam: 010, 1998.

- MVRDV. *Metacity Datatown*. Rotterdam: 010, 1999.

- Edgar Allan POE. *Nouvelles Histoires Extraordinaires*. (1857 - translation by Charles Baudelaire) Paris: Gallimard, 1974.

- Saskia SASSEN, *Globalization and its Discontents*. New York: The New York Press, 1998.

- Georg SIMMEL, *Philosophie de la modernité*. Paris: Payot, 1989.

- Ignasi de SOLA-MORALES, *Differences*. Cambridge (Mass.): MIT Press, 1996.

- Robert VENTURI, *Learning from Las Vegas*. Cambridge (Mass.): MIT Press, 1977.

- Paul VIRILIO, *L'espace critique*. Paris: Christian Bourgois, 1984.

- Paul VIRILIO, *L'esthétique de la disparition*. Paris: Christian Bourgois, 1984.

- Stefan ZWEIG, *Lander, stadte, landschaften*. Frankfurt: Fischer Taschenbuch Verlag, 1981.

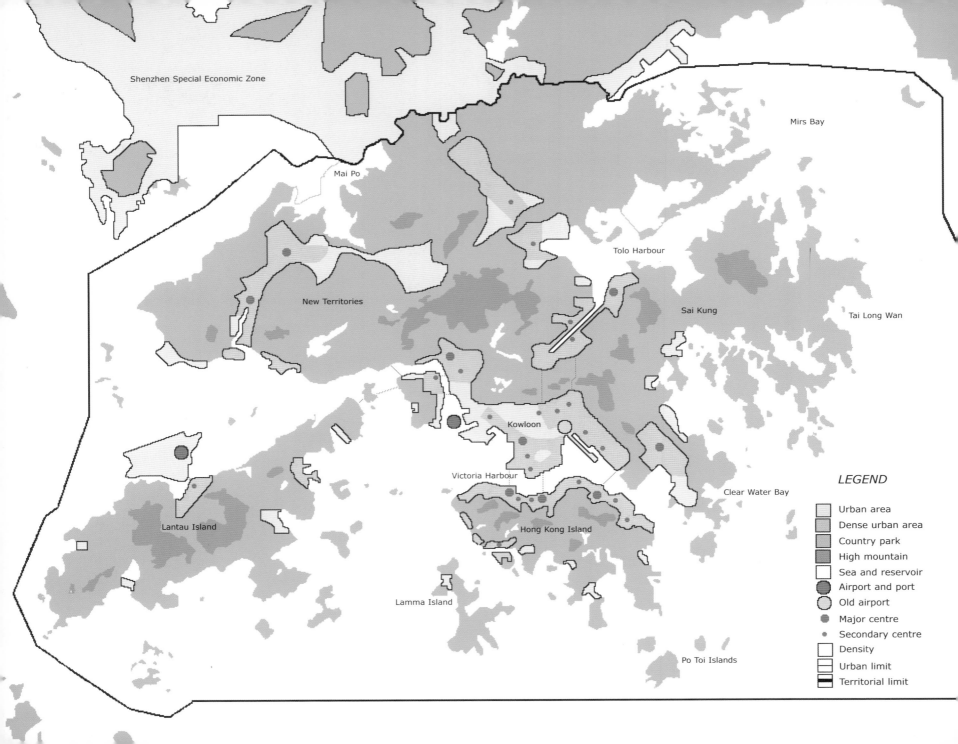

Shenzhen Special Economic Zone

Mirs Bay

Mai Po

Tolo Harbour

New Territories

Sai Kung

Tai Long Wan

Kowloon

Victoria Harbour

Clear Water Bay

Lantau Island

Hong Kong Island

Lamma Island

Po Toi Islands

LEGEND

Urban area
Dense urban area
Country park
High mountain
Sea and reservoir
Airport and port
Old airport
Major centre
Secondary centre
Density
Urban limit
Territorial limit

Maps & Places

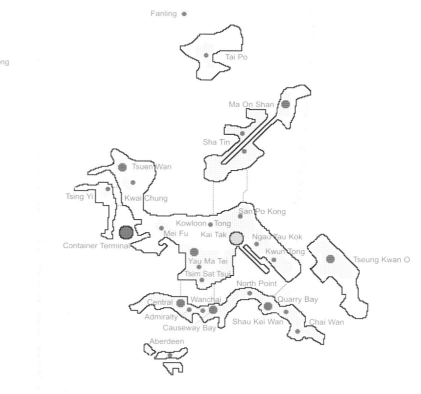

Lo Wu

Sheung Shui

Fanling

Yuen Long

Tai Po

Ma On Shan

Tuen Mun

Sha Tin

Tsuen Wan

Tsing Yi

Kwai Chung

San Po Kong

Kowloon Tong

Mei Fu

Kai Tak

Ngau Tau Kok

Container Terminal

Kwun Tong

Tseung Kwan O

Chek Lap Kok International Airport

Yau Ma Tei

Tsim Sat Tsui

North Point

Tung Chung

Central

Wanchai

Quarry Bay

Admiralty

Shau Kei Wan

Chai Wan

Causeway Bay

Aberdeen